DOMINICAN REPUBLIC

DOMINICAN REPUBLIC

Alexander Creed

CHELSEA HOUSE

3 5 7 9 8 6 4

Library of Congress Cataloging-in-Publication Data

Creed, Alexander.
  Dominican Republic.
  Includes index.
  Summary: Surveys the history, topography, people, and culture of the Dominican
Republic, with an emphasis on its current economy, industry, and place in the political
world.

    1. Dominican Republic. [1. Dominican Republic]
I. Title.
F1934.C74   1987   972.93   86-21597

ISBN 1-55546-163-8

Project Editor: Elizabeth L. Mauro
Associate Editor: Rafaela Ellis
Chief Copy Editor: Melissa R. Padovani
Art Director: Maureen McCafferty
Series Designer: Anita Noble
Project Coordinator: Kathleen P. Luczak
Production Manager: Brian A. Shulik

ACKNOWLEDGMENTS

The author and publishers are grateful to the following people and organizations for
information and photographs: Dominican Republic Tourism Office; Library of Congress; Organization of American States; Philadelphia Phillies/Ed Mahan, photographer; Antonio Rodriguez, photographer. Picture Research: Imagefinders, Inc.

Contents

UNITED STATES

ATLANTIC OCEAN

BAHAMAS

GULF OF MEXICO

PUERTO RICO

HAITI

MEXICO

CUBA

DOMINICAN
REPUBLIC

BELIZE

JAMAICA

HONDURAS

NICARAGUA

CARIBBEAN SEA

GUATEMALA
EL SALVADOR

PANAMA

COSTA RICA

VENEZUELA

COLOMBIA

ma R.

● Higüey

San Pedro
de Macorís

Santo Domingo

La Romana

N

This statue of Christopher Columbus honors the man who discovered the island

Introducing the Dominican Republic

During his first voyage to the New World, Christopher Columbus spotted the coral-edged coastline of Hispaniola, the second-largest island in the West Indies. "There is no more beautiful island in the world," he proclaimed. In 1492, Columbus established on this beautiful island the first permanent European settlement in the Americas. Although the Spanish settlers eventually neglected the Dominican Republic in favor of other lands, the country has since developed into a unique nation where diverse cultures have blended into one.

In 1496, Columbus's brother, Bartolome, founded the port city of Santo Domingo—the oldest city in the Western Hemisphere—on Hispaniola. In the 17th century, the island was divided into two countries, the Dominican Republic and Haiti. Today, Santo Domingo is the capital of the Dominican Republic.

The Dominican Republic occupies the eastern two-thirds of Hispaniola, and Haiti occupies the western third. Although they share an island, the two countries are culturally and ethnically different. Whereas the Haitians are French in tradition and African in descent, the 5.5 million Dominicans are Spanish in tradition and of both European and African descent.

Because it is located at the entrance to the Caribbean Sea, with convenient access to other island trading ports (most notably the once-rich ports of the Lesser Antilles), the Dominican Republic has had a troubled history. For centuries, foreign powers battled for control of the country's ports and sea lanes. At various times, it has been ruled by Spain, France, and Haiti. In 1844, it gained its independence. Until 1962, however, the country was governed by a series of dictators who cared little for the people's welfare. Poverty

and unemployment soared. Today, the Dominican Republic's government is a democracy, and its new leaders are trying to solve the many problems created by years of repressive rule.

The Dominican Republic is one of the oldest countries in the New World, but it is only beginning to develop economically and politically. Although it faces many financial and social problems, the tiny island nation retains the beauty that charmed Christopher Columbus.

Columbus spotted Hispaniola's coastline during his first voyage to the New World

11

The Land

The Dominican Republic is roughly the size of the states of Vermont and New Hampshire combined—about 18,816 square miles (48,921 square kilometers). Located just south of the Tropic of Capricorn, it is bordered on the north by the Atlantic Ocean, on the south by the Caribbean Sea, and on the east by the Mona Passage, which separates the island from Puerto Rico.

The Dominican Republic's varied terrain features both the highest and the lowest points in the Caribbean. Mountain ranges

Mountain ranges cover much of the Dominican Republic

cover nearly three-fifths of the nation, making it one of the most mountainous lands in the West Indies. Still, it is possible to drive from an icy mountain to a barren desert plain in just a few hours.

Four mountain ranges grace the Dominican Republic. The largest range, the Cordillera Central, runs from east to west through the center of the country. Its pine-covered slopes reach some of the highest elevations in the Caribbean. At 10,490 feet (3,197 meters), Pico Duarte in the heart of the Cordillera Central is the highest point in the West Indies.

Another range, the Cordillera Septentrional, runs along the northern coast of the Republic. Made of limestone and shale, the mountains in this range are narrower and lower than those in the

Central range. The highest peak in the Cordillera Septentrional is only 4,000 feet (1,220 meters).

Stretching across the southwest, the mountains of the Sierra de Neiba and Sierra de Bahoruco are even lower than the Cordillera Septentrional. Several mining companies operate in the Sierra de Bahoruco range, which is important for its deposits of red bauxite, a mineral used to make aluminum products.

Between the Cordillera Central and the Cordillera Septentrional lies the fertile Cibao Valley, known as "the food basket of the Republic." The Cibao contains 150 square miles (390 square kilometers) of the country's best agricultural land. The valley was not always as productive as it is today. Its dry western section was once home to cacti and thornbushes. Thanks to a government irrigation program, however, crops now grow, despite an average annual rainfall of only 20 inches (500 millimeters).

Lush plants thrive in Santo Domingo's Botanical Gardens

Known as the Vega Real (or Royal Meadow), the Cibao's eastern portion is the most fertile plain in the West Indies. Coffee is the area's major crop, although tobacco, fruit, beans, rice, corn, tomatoes, and eggplant also grow there. Most of the crops grown in the valley are sold inside the Dominican Republic, but some coffee and sugar cane are exported. Whereas the valley between the Cordillera Central and the Cordillera Septentrional is the most fertile in the Dominican Republic, the area between the Sierra de Neiba and the Sierra de Bahoruco is the most barren. This region, known as the Cul-de-Sac, has a desert climate. Crops cannot grow here, and even people have difficulty surviving. Only 10 percent of Dominicans live in the area.

Most of the Cul-de-Sac is below sea level, sometimes as much as 144 feet (44 meters). It contains the lowest point in the West Indies, and scientists believe that it was most likely covered by the Caribbean Sea in prehistoric times. The only lake in the region is also the largest and saltiest in the country: the 25-mile-long (40 kilometer) Lago de Enriquillo, or Enriquillo's Lake. It is home to many ferocious American crocodiles, which reach an average length of 21 feet (7 meters).

The Dominican Republic has four major rivers: the Yaque del Norte, the Yaque del Sur, the Yuma, and the Artibonito. Important sources of fresh water, these rivers provide drinking water for Dominicans and irrigation for their crops. They also help prevent floods by draining excess rainfall from the mountains. The Artibonito, the longest river on Hispaniola, drains rainfall from a large portion of the western Republic before it flows into Haiti.

This waterfall is only one of the Republic's many natural wonders

Climate

Although the Dominican Republic is located in the tropics, its climate is relatively mild. Both the mountains and the cool easterly breezes known as trade winds keep temperatures from becoming excessively high. Along the coast, temperatures usually average between 75° and 80° Fahrenheit (25° and 27° Centigrade). At higher elevations, however, temperatures can be quite cold. It is common for winter temperatures in the mountain regions to drop to the freezing point. Because these frigid conditions prevent the growth of coffee and other sensitive crops, plant life at high elevations is similar to that found on the North American mainland. Visitors to the Pico Duarte are often surprised to see entire forests of pine and oak—trees most often found at northern latitudes.

Because of its Caribbean location, the Dominican Republic is subject to hurricanes in August and September. Fortunately, these storms seldom hit the island directly. But when they do strike, they can be extremely destructive. Older Dominicans remember the 1930 hurricane that devastated Santo Domingo, leaving many buildings in ruins.

During the rainy season—from May through November—rainfall averages about 60 inches (1,500 millimeters) a year in Santo Domingo and other southern locations. In the mountains, annual rainfall averages more than 100 inches (2,500 mm). In the barren Cul-de-Sac, only 50 inches (1,300 mm) are recorded each year. Surprisingly, humidity is moderate throughout most of the country, although some below-sea-level locations are occasionally muggy.

Although no major earthquakes have shaken the Dominican Republic in recent years, many towns along the northern coast are subject to frequent tremors. However, most Dominicans are used to these minor quakes.

Salt cliffs add to the Republic's rugged terrain

Native blooms, such as this water lily, cover the island

Plant and Animal Life

The Dominican Republic is home to a wide variety of plants. The most common plant is sugar cane, but vegetation also includes grasses, small shrubs, and scrubby trees. Dense forests of pine and broadleaf evergreen are found in areas where rainfall is heavy.

Forests cover about half the country, with tropical rain forests covering most of the land at lower elevations. These rain forests yield a great many products: dyewoods, edible fruits, and woods used for cabinetmaking. The most abundant trees in the rain forests are mahogany, satinwood, ebony, lignum vitae, cedar, and juniper. Fruit-bearing trees include star apple, soursop, cashew, wild pepper, wild guava, and calabash. The rain forests also contain royal palm, a particularly beautiful tree native to Hispaniola.

Equally important are the pine forests, which cover nearly

2,500 square miles (6,500 square kilometers) of the Republic. Forests of yellow pine are found in the higher elevations of the Cordillera Central. These trees, similar to the yellow pines of the southeastern United States, have long been considered the nation's most valuable untapped resource.

In addition to native vegetation, a variety of trees and shrubs imported from all over the world cover the island. Eucalyptus trees from Australia, almond trees from India, breadfruit trees from various Pacific islands, and coffee trees from Africa can all be found in the Dominican Republic. Citrus, mango, banana, coconut, rose apple, cacao and papaya—all from South and Central America—also bloom on Dominican soil. Big cities and small towns alike are adorned with the blossoms of bougainvillea (a flowering tropical vine), white angel's trumpet, and poinsettia—all imported from neighboring Caribbean islands.

Although plant life is lush and varied, animal life is rather limited. Dangerous alligators and crocodiles breed in the nation's lakes and rivers, but other reptiles are few and relatively harmless. Lizards, most notably edible iguanas, are found in the deserts. There are no poisonous snakes on the island, because of the many mongooses. Small, slender, meat-eating mammals, mongooses feed on birds, eggs, and small animals, controlling the Republic's reptile and rodent population. The only rodents that the mongooses do not eat are agouti (short-haired, short-eared, rabbit-like animals that chew through sugar cane) and *solendon* (tiny, insect-eating creatures with long snouts and hairless, scaly tails).

Insects thrive in the rain-drenched Republic. Most are harm-

The waters surrounding the Dominican Republic are home to many kinds of fish, shellfish, and reptiles, including this sea turtle

less, but mosquitos carrying malaria—a tropical disease—occasionally breed in the lowlands, as do tarantulas, scorpions and poisonous centipedes.

Many beautiful and exotic birds live in the Dominican Republic. Brightly colored parrots inhabit the forests, and pelicans and ducks live on the coasts near the water. Pink flamingos can be spotted in the Neiba Valley, although they are not as plentiful as they once were. Pigeons, nightingales, swallows, and melodic musician birds also live in the forests and along the coasts.

Many kinds of fish and shellfish thrive in the waters surrounding the Republic. Shrimp, mullet, red snapper, turtles, and a species of small oyster inhabit offshore waters. Many kinds of fish can also be found in Lago de Enriquillo, although its increasing saltiness may soon kill some freshwater species.

The most unusual sea creature found in the area is the gentle manatee, also known as the sea cow. After years of being hunted for its oil, hide, and flesh, this mammal is now an endangered species. Manatees grow from 8 to 13 feet (2.5 to 4 meters) long and resemble large seals. But although they appear fearsome, they are actually awkward, harmless creatures that dine on weeds and water grasses. On still nights along the rivers, a manatee's crunching teeth and flapping lips can be heard up to 200 yards (60 meters) away.

The History

The island of Hispaniola became known to Europe in the late 15th century when it was discovered by Christopher Columbus. He literally stumbled onto the island in December of 1492, when his flagship, the *Santa Maria*, ran ashore on the Atlantic coast of what is now Haiti. Columbus and his crew found a lush, tropical island inhabited by primitive tribesmen whom Columbus called "Indians" because he believed he had sailed from Europe to the East Indies.

The *Santa Maria* was wrecked, and its crew could not return to Spain—there was not enough room on the remaining ships. Columbus constructed a small fort named *Navidad* (Christmas) for the men who had to be left behind. He thought the Indians were friendly, but when he returned the following year he found that they had destroyed his fort and killed his crew.

Nevertheless, Columbus established Isabella, the first colony in the New World, on Hispaniola in 1493. When the settlers discovered gold and silver and tried to force the Indians to give up their land, war broke out. This war lasted for almost 50 years, and when it ended, the entire native population of Hispaniola—approximately 100,000 people—had been killed by the Spanish settlers. From the beginning, it had been an uneven match. The Indians were

Christopher Columbus claimed the island of Hispaniola for Spain in December 1492, as this painting shows

equipped only with primitive weapons, while the Spanish had guns and other sophisticated battle gear.

Three years after Columbus established Isabella, his brother, Bartolome, founded the settlement of Santo Domingo (originally called Santiago de Guzman) on the island's southern coast. Located on a safe, protected harbor, the city became the administrative capital for all of Spain's colonies in the Americas. In the early 1500s, Christopher Columbus's son, Diego, built a lavish palace in Santo Domingo. This palace, the Alcazar, was the first European fortress in the Americas.

Hispaniola prospered for several decades, especially after Bartolome Columbus, a poor administrator, was removed from the governorship. The island became less important, however, after Spain began to colonize nearby Mexico and Peru. Most of the original settlers eventually left for other, richer lands. By the end of the 16th century, Spain had virtually abandoned the western end of Hispaniola. To preserve the colony, settlers were officially encouraged to abandon their farms in the interior and congregate around Santo Domingo and in the eastern portion of the island.

In the mid-1500s, a number of European nations began exploring Hispaniola. Adventurers from France, Holland, and England converged on the island in pursuit of riches. In 1563, British explorer Sir John Hawkins arrived with African slaves for the sugar plantations outside of Santo Domingo. Another Briton, Sir Francis Drake, paid a much less welcome visit three years later, when he seized Santo Domingo. Drake pillaged the colony, leaving with some 25,000 gold ducats (European coins) and an array of other treasures.

Sir Francis Drake pillaged the colony of Santo Domingo

Touissant l'Ouverture seized eastern Hispaniola in 1801

While England was concentrating on eastern Hispaniola, France was establishing a large community on the other side of the island. By the middle of the 17th century, the French-owned Company of the West Indies had taken control of western Hispaniola, and in 1697 Spain gave this region to France under the Treaty of Ryswick. The French colony—known at first as St. Domingue and later as Haiti—grew and prospered, while the rest of the island declined in both population and importance. In 1795, Spain assigned the entire island to France in the Treaty of Basel.

At the turn of the 19th century, a revolution against French rule took place in Haiti, which proclaimed itself independent. Then, in 1801, Haitian leader Toussaint l'Ouverture seized the eastern portion of the island as well. French emperor Napoleon quickly sent an army to recapture it for France. Although Napoleon's troops failed to conquer Haiti, the eastern end of Hispaniola was returned to French control. The people of the region, however, retained the heritage of three centuries as a colony of Spain.

In 1809, Spanish nationalist Juan Sanchez Ramirez led a revolt that restored Spanish rule to the eastern part of the island. But Spain's sovereignty was challenged in 1821 when Creoles (people of mixed Spanish and African descent) staged a revolt in hopes of uniting Santo Domingo with the Republic of Colombia. The Creole revolt was successful, and a new government headed by José Nuñez de Caceres was installed.

Creole domination of the colony did not last long, however. Haiti once again invaded and captured the eastern end of Hispaniola. The Haitians ruled the entire island until the 1840s, when European-educated patriot Juan Pablo Duarte (for whom Pico Duarte is named) started an uprising that expelled the Haitians from the eastern portion of the island. On February 27, 1844, independence was declared in Santo Domingo, and the Dominican Republic was born.

Independence and Beyond

From the very beginning, the going was tough for the independent Republic. A struggle between the country's first two presidents, Pedro Santana and Buenaventura Báez, along with the ever-present fear of another Haitian invasion, created unstable conditions. Tensions were so great that the Republic asked a number of foreign powers to consider taking it over. The United States, France, and Great Britain agreed to protect the nation from Haiti, but each refused to assume complete responsibility. The country that for years had fought to fend off foreign domination suddenly found itself unwanted by foreign powers.

In 1861, Spain was finally persuaded to reinstate its sovereignty over the Dominican Republic. Although the move was made at the request of their president, the Dominican people were clearly opposed to the Spanish presence. The occupational forces, hampered by outbreaks of yellow fever, were unable to maintain order. In 1865, Spain finally abandoned the colony. Shortly thereafter, William Cazneau and Joseph Fabens, two adventurers who had business interests in the area, proposed that the United States take control of the Dominican Republic. Although this idea was supported by both the Dominican president and United States President Ulysses S. Grant, opposition in the U.S. Congress prevented such a move.

Extreme disorder reigned on the island until 1882, when Ulises Heureaux took control of the government. Heureaux, a black man whom the Dominicans called "Lilis," ruled in a strict and often violent manner, but his cruel regime gave the Republic its first real period of stability and prosperity. Aided by financial support from the United States, sugar production increased, and the economy appeared to be growing. Unfortunately, the nation's foreign debt also grew during this period. To gain capital, the government sold large amounts of bonds in Europe, then wasted the proceeds.

The country entered another period of civil strife in 1899, when President Heureaux was assassinated. Debts continued to increase, and soon several European governments began to demand payment on their bonds. In 1904, General Carlos F. Morales was sworn in as president, and he promptly asked the United States to help the Republic clear its foreign debt. The U. S.

persuaded creditors to accept scaled-down settlements, thus giving the Dominican government more money for public projects.

The Republic seemed to be doing well until 1911, when the assassination of newly elected President Ramón Cáceres brought another period of chaos. Colonel Alfredo Victoria, a military leader, installed his uncle, Eladio Victoria, as president, enraging other political leaders. Hoping to avert a revolution, the United States persuaded the Dominicans to elect Adolfo Nouel, a Catholic clergyman, as president. Monsignor Nouel's presidency lasted only a few months. He resigned when he realized that he could not control the real leaders of the country—the military commanders.

Shortly after Nouel stepped down, a civil war broke out. The United States intervened and restored peace, but only temporarily. Soon, fighting broke out again—so intensely that President Woodrow Wilson proposed sending the United States Marines to quell the violence. That never became necessary, however. The Dominicans

Ships dock by Santo Domingo's customhouse

28

The Republic's flag flies proudly

agreed to solve their differences and to elect a temporary president until formal elections could be held.

By 1915, a large national debt had accumulated, and the Republic again turned to the United States for assistance. The U. S. asked President Juan Isidro Jiménez to give an American controller authority over other expenditures, including tax revenues. President Jiménez, concerned with more urgent problems within the country, rejected this proposal.

President Jiménez's prime concern was to free himself from the control of Desiderio Arias, the minister of war. Arias, the most powerful figure in the Dominican government, openly defied Jiménez and eventually forced him to resign. The United States saw Arias as a threat to its efforts to establish a stable government in the Republic, and sent the marines to Santo Domingo and to other island ports to ensure peace. When the new Dominican president, Francisco Henríquez y Carbajal, refused to make financial reforms, the United States took full military control of the Republic.

Some Dominicans bitterly resented the United States presence in their country. Although the American occupation brought progress in education, public health, and economic development, it also brought military rule, censorship of the press, and economic exploitation by American business firms. After four years, President Woodrow Wilson announced that the marines would be withdrawn if Dominican leaders would cooperate in establishing the proposed reforms. The leaders steadfastly refused, forcing the United States to abandon this condition and end its occupation in 1924.

For the next six years, the Republic enjoyed a rare period of peace. But in 1930, problems flared when President Horatio Vasquez tried to get reelected. During the turmoil that followed, General Rafael Leonidas Trujillo Molina seized the presidency.

Trujillo (center) ruled brutally until his assassination in 1961

The Trujillo Years

When Trujillo took office, the Dominicans were suffering the effects of two economic catastrophes. One was a strong hurricane that virtually destroyed Santo Domingo and other coastal towns, and the other was a drastic drop in the price of sugar, the Republic's chief export. The new president gained the support of the Dominican people by quickly rebuilding the capital city, increasing exports, expanding public highways, and settling a border dispute with neighboring Haiti. By the late 1940s, Trujillo had even managed to pay off the country's enormous foreign debt.

But all this progress was not without a price. Soon it was clear that Trujillo had become an absolute dictator. He began to make repressive rules, outlawing political opposition and controlling every aspect of Dominican political and economic life. He placed all agricultural production under the control of his family—soon it was difficult to separate the country's assets from Trujillo's personal wealth. Although Trujillo was noted for his personal thriftiness, he allowed his family and friends to spend public money freely.

Political and moral corruption pervaded the government. Trujillo placed figureheads in powerful positions to give the appearance of a democracy, but retained absolute power. He renamed the capital Ciudad Trujillo (Trujillo City) in honor of himself. He even erected public signs honoring "God and Trujillo." His secret police force intimidated or eliminated all political opponents. Although he had hoped to become known as "El Benefactor" (The Benefactor), more often than not he was called "The Goat" by the oppressed Dominicans.

31

For more than two decades, Trujillo enjoyed absolute power. In the late 1950s, however, his influence began to wane. In 1959, a group of Dominican exiles based in Cuba attempted to overthrow him. Although this endeavor failed, Trujillo's government became the object of scorn throughout the free world, and in 1960 the Organization of American States (OAS) expelled the Republic.

On May 30, 1961, Trujillo was assassinated by members of his own army as he drove along a boulevard in Santo Domingo. When he spotted his attackers, he leaped out of his car, drew his pistol, and shouted, "Come on, let's fight." Moments later, he was dead.

After 1961

After Trujillo's death, the task of establishing a stable government fell to a generation of Dominicans that had never known true democracy. Every part of Dominican society had its own idea about how the nation should be run. Military officials wanted the army to regain control. The social elite, the aristocrats who had been persecuted by Trujillo, hoped to regain its former position of political power. The urban middle class yearned for a free, democratic society. And the rural peasants, who cared little about politics, wanted only to improve their financial condition.

Although Trujillo's successor, Joaquín Balaguer, attempted to make the government more democratic, he was ousted in 1962. Later that year, Juan Bosch, a writer and professor who had spent most of his life in exile, was elected president. Bosch's liberal policies infuriated conservatives, however, and the military took over in a nonviolent coup. The armed forces ruled until 1965.

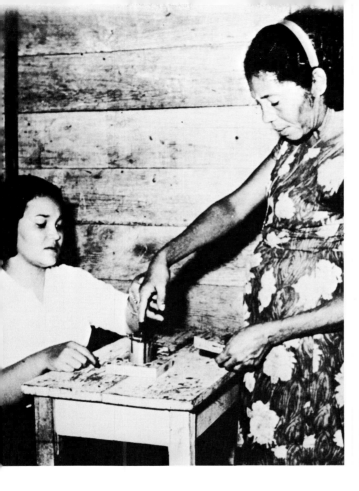

To prevent double voting, this voter dips her finger in ink

In the spring of 1965, young military officers hoping to reinstate the deposed Bosch started a civil war. The United States, distressed by reports of Communist activity among the military, sent a sizable force to stop the war and restore stability. This action was criticized by the Organization of American States, which gave military command of the Republic to an international peacekeeping force.

When tensions eased, a temporary president was installed and new elections were held. In 1966, former president Joaquín Balaguer defeated Juan Bosch. Although Balaguer had once served under Trujillo, he had become respected as a moderate conservative.

During the early years of his administration, President Balaguer tried to unite the various warring groups in the Republic. He took members of the opposition party into his government and halted military interference. He also took action to help the business community and the large rural population. For the first time, Dominicans were given a taste of prosperity without the terror of dictatorship. Balaguer was reelected in 1970 and 1974.

In 1978, however, Balaguer was defeated by Antonio Guzman, a candidate of the Dominican Revolutionary Party (PRD). During Guzman's term in office, the military planned another coup, but retreated under pressure from the United States. Dismayed by the instability of his government, Guzman was unable to achieve any important reforms.

Guzman also had problems controlling the Republic's soaring debt. He was such a poor administrator, in fact, that the PRD did not nominate him again. Another PRD candidate, Salvador Jorge Blanco, was elected in 1982. Blanco was plagued by financial problems for the four years he was in office. Although he reduced inflation from 38 percent to 14 percent, unemployment soared. He was not able to institute any significant reforms, and when the 1986 presidential campaign began, his party nominated another candidate.

The PRD's candidate, Senate President Jacobo Majluta, was pitted against former President Joaquín Balaguer of the Social Christian Reform party and Juan Bosch (also a former president) of the Marxist Dominican Liberation party. The campaign was marred by sporadic violence in which 15 people were killed. The election was so close that it took ten days for the election board to proclaim a winner. Finally, the 78-year-old Balaguer was declared the victor with 41.6 percent of the vote. Although blind and frail, he vowed to implement new programs to help the slumping Dominican economy.

The violence that scarred the 1986 elections worried many Dominicans who had hoped that such problems were part of their country's past. During the campaign, incumbent President Blanco said that the chaos reminded him "of the days when the democratic process was constantly threatened" in the Dominican Republic. Although the people are committed to democracy, it may take some time before the violent patterns of the past are erased.

Daily Life and Religion

Although the culture and language of the Dominican Republic are Spanish, the Dominican people are a mixture of races. About 70 percent of them are of combined Spanish and African heritage. Another 20 percent are direct descendants of African slaves brought to the island beginning in the 16th century, and the remaining 10 percent are white, primarily of Spanish descent.

For years, Dominicans of European descent dominated business and political affairs. When Trujillo seized power in 1930, he took away many of the land-holdings and most of the political power of this elite class. Since his death, the elite has attempted to regain its former position of power. The result has been renewed hostility between the upper and lower classes.

Recently, a small middle class of farmers and tradesmen has emerged in the Republic. While some are immigrants from Europe and the Middle East, most are former members of the lower class who have worked their way up the economic ladder.

At the very bottom of the ladder is the lower class, comprised mostly of displaced farmers who represent the largest percentage of the country's population. Exploited by landowners, the lower class has not been allowed much of a role in Dominican affairs.

A young couple enjoying the merengue, the national dance

Illiteracy and unemployment are high among its members, many of whom live in extreme poverty.

Many impoverished country people were recruited into the armed forces during the Trujillo era, but this did little to curb the nation's poverty problem. Recently, farm workers formed a peasant movement to campaign against persecution by employers. Now, more people are aware of the plight of the poor, and the government is making attempts to curb poverty.

Dominicans are very conscious of their racial backgrounds, and most are proud of their diversity. But even though open discrimination is rare, many people believe that secret prejudice guides Dominican life. Most blacks are confined to the lower classes, and job opportunities for people of pure African descent are limited.

Cottages with thatched roofs dot the rural landscape

Rural Life

Most Dominicans live in cool, shady mountain villages. On the small farms that dot the landscape, chickens and geese scamper around the barnyard while goats and donkeys graze in the fields. Coffee shrubs with ripe, red berries and orange trees heavy with fruit line the unpaved streets.

The residents of these villages live in small wooden farmhouses. Some of these country cottages have thatched roofs; others have roofs made of corrugated tin. Many homes are painted in bright colors—aquamarine (a light blue-green) is particularly popular.

Most country farmhouses have only one room, which serves as a living room during the day and as a bedroom for the entire family at night. Floors are usually made of packed dirt. Few rural homes have kitchens. Instead, meals are prepared in separate cookhouses that have slotted sides to let out the smoke. This arrangement helps keep the farmhouses cool.

In a typical mountain village, an unpaved road leads to the center of town. Most activity centers around one street or square. A general store, a butcher shop, the church, and a one-table pool hall or small cafe are usually located in the village center. Although village life has remained almost unchanged for generations, some small towns now have modern medical clinics and other conveniences.

Religion

Religion is so important to Dominicans that the Bible is in the center of the Republic's coat of arms. Because its first settlers were from Catholic Spain, the nation has been predominately Roman Catholic since colonial times. It has been the site of many Catholic firsts in the New World: the first Catholic Mass (1493); the first archbishop (1547); and the first cathedral, the Cathedral of Santa Maria de la Menor (1541).

Dominicans respect the church, and the government wholeheartedly supports church activities. Although approximately 95 percent of the population is Roman Catholic, the constitution of the Republic proclaims freedom of worship for its people. Indeed,

The New World's first Catholic cathedral was built in the Republic

most Dominicans are extremely tolerant of other religions. Two percent of the population is Protestant, and about .02 percent—roughly 1,000 people—is Jewish. The rest either are nonbelievers or practice some other faith. In rural areas, voodoo is sometimes practiced. Although most Catholics frown on conversion to other faiths and many believe that voodoo is sacrilegious, neither Protestants nor Jews are persecuted.

Each religion plays an important part in the lives of its followers, and the Dominican people cannot be understood without first examining their religious beliefs.

Catholicism

The overwhelming majority of the Dominican people are Catholics. Even those who don't uphold the formal doctrines of the church describe themselves as *muy Catolico* (very Catholic). *Campesinos* (country people) are generally considered more devout than urbanites, and Catholicism is particularly strong in the rural Cibao Valley. Among city-dwellers, Catholicism is strongest in the middle class.

In keeping with the Dominicans' strong ties with Catholicism, shrines, churches, and religious artifacts abound on the island. The most important shrine is dedicated to Nuestra Señora de la Merced (Our Lady of Mercy), whom the early Spanish settlers believed protected Hispaniola. According to legend, Columbus and his men were awakened one night by an Indian attack. Almost defeated, Columbus's men placed a cross in the soil; a vision of the Virgin Mary immediately appeared. The Indians were so frightened that they allowed Columbus and his troops to win the battle.

*A view of the main altar of a
Santo Domingo cathedral*

The shrine of Nuestra Señora is said to be built on the spot where Columbus planted the cross that night. In front of it stands the tree trunk from which he supposedly cut the wood for the cross. The shrine itself contains two splinters believed to be remnants of the cross. (A larger piece of the cross is stored in a cathedral in Santo Domingo.) Located at Santo Cerro (Holy Hill), the shrine is perched on a spectacular mountainside overlooking the Vega Real. Many Dominicans believe that a visit to it will cure them of illness.

Another Madonna, La Altagracia, or the Virgin of the Highest Grace, has become a revered religious symbol. Many Dominicans believe that La Altagracia appeared before a Dominican farmer. According to legend, a mysterious pilgrim—later said to be one of Christ's Apostles—arrived in the town of Higuey and asked the father of a sick girl for food and shelter. The farmer obliged, and when the pilgrim left the following day, he gave his host a small picture of La Altagracia. As soon as the man looked at the picture, his sick daughter was miraculously healed.

41

Since then, many Dominicans have worshipped La Altagracia. A church was built beneath the orange tree where the farmer and his daughter first gazed upon the picture of the Virgin. Each year, many people flock to Higuey to visit the site of the miracle. Many Dominicans display pictures of the Virgin wearing a crown and looking at the Christ Child. In 1922, La Altagracia was named the official patroness of the Dominican Republic.

A number of other religious figures have special significance to Dominican Catholics. In Bayaguana, people flock to see the Cristo de Bayaguana, an ancient statue of Christ. In Santo Domingo, a famous statue of St. Anthony is believed to have the power to cause earthquakes if it is removed from its pedestal. And Our Lady of Fatima, who first appeared to three Portuguese children in 1917, is said to have performed many miracles since pilgrims carried a statue of her through the Dominican countryside in 1940.

Evidence of Catholic devotion can be seen all over the country in the form of *calvarios*, small groups of crosses representing the three crosses of Calvary. Very common in rural areas, they are most often found along roadsides, at crossroads, or near the doorways of houses. The calvarios are a sign of welcome to weary pilgrims. They also serve as prayer stations in religious processions, called *rosarios*, formed by Dominicans who need rain, want to cure a common illness, or have other problems. At the head of the procession, a leader carries an image of the Virgin Mary or a saint. The leader is followed by a song leader, who carries a large rosary of polished wood. Musicians playing guitars, accordions, tambourines, flutes, and drums march behind, followed by the remaining

Calvarios serve as prayer stations in religious processions

participants—usually women, children, and elderly men. Many Dominicans believe that in order for a rosario to be effective, no one may leave the procession until it has returned to its starting point.

Dominican Catholicism is often interspersed with superstitious practices. Rural peasants wear religious charms to ward off sickness or misfortune. The most common superstition involves a series of mystical formulas called *orasiones*. Orasiones can be used to bring good luck to a new adventure, but most often they are used to ward off the "evil eye" (malevolent influences) or to cure illness. Another superstitious practice is the *ensalmo*, a chant used by older Dominican women to cure disease.

Other common Dominican superstitions include the following: if a crab is seen scurrying far from water, rain will come; if an

St. Michael battles the devil in this 16th-century sculpture

unmarried woman consents to be a godmother, she will never marry; if a couple marries in November, their marriage will be a failure; and if a wedding guest wears black, the couple will have bad luck.

Catholic feasts and saint's days are an important part of Dominican life, often celebrated with huge festivals and parades. The major religious holidays are the Feast of the Circumcision, the Feast of the Epiphany, Our Lady of Altagracia Day, Saint Joseph's Day, the Feast of the Assumption, Our Lady of Mercedes Day, All Saints Day, the Feast of the Immaculate Conception, Christmas, and Easter.

Christmas celebrations usually begin on Christmas Eve with a midnight Mass. Special dinners and dances are held during the following week. Dominicans do not traditionally exchange gifts or decorate trees on Christmas day. Instead, gifts are exchanged on the Feast of the Epiphany (January 6th), the day that the Magi brought their offerings to the infant Jesus. On that day, children receive gifts brought not by Santa Claus but by the Magi.

Most Dominicans consider a church wedding very important, and most also have their children baptized. Even those who rarely go to church would never embark on a trip without first being blessed by the local priest.

Priests and Nuns

Currently, there is a shortage of parishes and priests in the Republic. Only about 650 churches and 300 priests serve more than 5,000,000 Catholics. The Diocese of Santo Domingo has a great many priests, but smaller dioceses have very few. Although the ratio of priests to the population has decreased since the early part of the 20th century, the actual number of religious servants has increased. Many new churches have been built since the late 1950s. In fact, between 1950 and 1960, the increase in churches and clergymen in the Republic was greater than in any other Caribbean country.

Many of the nuns who serve in the Republic teach at local schools

Many of the priests who serve the Republic are not Dominicans. Most are from Spain. A typical priest has a college education and three or four years of seminary training. Because the Republic has only one Catholic university, most of the priests work in parishes.

Aside from their role as spiritual leaders, Catholic priests provide leadership in political, economic, and social affairs. Most recently they have promoted labor seminars and consumers' cooperatives in rural regions. Many work for social justice and reform in an effort to rid the country of its enormous poverty problem.

In addition to priests, more than 800 nuns of more than 24 orders serve in the Republic. Church-operated hospitals and charitable organizations are staffed by members of the religious community. Nuns nurse at hospitals and teach at local schools.

Protestantism

Protestant missionaries first arrived in the Republic in the late 19th century. Since then, Protestants of more than 20 denominations have established dozens of churches. Although they make up only 2 percent of the population, they have gained respect and stature over the years. Relations between the Catholic church and the Protestant churches have been cordial.

Some provinces on the east coast actually have more Protestants than Catholics. Many of the nation's Protestants are immigrants. Others—chiefly women and rural people—are Catholics who have converted to Protestantism.

Because the new constitution guarantees freedom of worship,

The ornate interior of a typical Santo Domingo cathedral

Dominican Protestants are not discriminated against. Under the Trujillo regime, however, many were subject to harassment. In 1957, Trujillo went so far as to expel all Jehovah's Witnesses from the country because they were politically neutral. Since Trujillo's assassination, however, the relationship between the Catholic church and the two leading Protestant sects—the Protestant Episcopal church and the Dominican Evangelical church—has been a friendly one.

A number of other Protestant sects operate missions in the Dominican Republic. Among them are the Free Methodist church, the African Methodist Episcopal church, the Seventh-Day Adventists, the Assemblies of God, the Christian Mission in Many Lands, the Church of God, and the Evangelical Mennonite church.

Judaism

More than 1,000 people in the Dominican Republic follow the Jewish faith. The Republic's Jews arrived in the country recently; most of them immigrated before World War II to escape Hitler. Nearly all of them settled in Santo Domingo and Sousa. Today, there are two synagogues in the capital city, one Orthodox (adhering strictly to the ancient laws of the Torah) and the other Conservative (allowing certain deviations from ancient codes). Services are held in Hebrew and Yiddish in the former synagogue, and in Hebrew and German in the latter.

Voodoo

A number of rural Dominicans belong to religious cults. The Laborista cult is centered in the tiny village of Palma Sola in the San Juan Province, and the Brotherhood of the Conga is dispersed throughout the country. But by far the best-known cult is voodoo, introduced to the Republic many years ago by Haitian descendants of African slaves.

Most of the African slaves brought to the Dominican Republic and Haiti came from the Dahomey region, where "voodoo" is the word for god. In other dialects voodoo is known as *vodun, voudou* or *vaudoux*. Considered by many to be a primitive practice, voodoo is actually highly structured, with a complicated set of rules.

In the Dominican Republic, voodoo is most often practiced by the blacks along the Haitian border, far removed from the mainstream of Dominican society. Although freedom of belief is respected, both the government and the majority of Dominicans consider voodoo to be anti-Catholic. Therefore, it is usually practiced secretly.

Male voodoo priests are called *hungans*, and female priests are known as *mambus*. Practitioners believe these priests can cure illnesses caused by magic or by the *loa* (voodoo gods who posses worshippers), but they cannot cure any disease sent by God. Voodooists also believe that hungans and mambus can predict the future. No important decision or family rite is attempted without first consulting a voodoo priest.

Voodoo cultists worship nature gods and family gods. They believe that nature gods control the external world, and worship each god at a particular time of the year in a special temple. They believe that family gods, the souls of dead ancestors, become more powerful with time. To ensure that the spirits of dead relatives don't become angry, voodooists plan elaborate funeral rites and memorial ceremonies.

The cultists also believe they can control personal forces and the soul through magic rituals and charms. In one ritual, known as *Fa—a*, a person throws 16 palm kernels in the air and interprets the pattern in which they fall. The powers of magical charms are thought to come from three sources: *Legba*, the middle man between the cultist and the gods; the Earth Gods; and the "little folk of the forests," fairy-like creatures who intercede in earthly affairs.

Government

During the 20th century, the Dominican Republic has been governed under a succession of constitutions. Unfortunately, powerful military and political leaders have frequently ignored the Dominican people's rights. Constitutional procedures have been observed since 1966, but the enormous power of the military leaders has made it difficult for the civilian government to ensure civil rights.

The Dominican government is made up of three branches: the executive, the legislative, and the judicial. The executive branch is headed by a president elected to a four-year term. The president governs with the advice and consent of the legislative branch, made up of a Senate and a Chamber of Deputies. Senators and deputies are also elected to four-year terms. The judicial branch of the government is headed by a Supreme Court, whose members are appointed by the president.

The Republic is divided into 26 provinces. The governor of each province is appointed by the president. City and town officials, including a mayor and a city or town council, are chosen in general elections.

In the United States, two major political parties, Republican and Democratic, influence the government. But in the Dominican

The Bible figures prominently in the Republic's coat of arms

Republic, at least six major political parties have a say in how the country is run.

For more than 30 years, from 1930 to 1961, the government was in the hands of the Dominican party. Headed by President Trujillo, the Dominican party tolerated no opposition. No other parties were allowed to exist. After Trujillo's assassination, however, the party was disbanded and a number of new political groups were formed.

Immediately after Trujillo's government collapsed, the moderate Reformist party took control. In the late 1970s, other parties sprang into power. The Dominican Revolutionary party—a social democratic group—won both the 1978 and 1982 elections. The Dominican Liberation party is also powerful, although it lost by a wide margin in the 1982 elections. Other political parties include the Revolutionary Social Christian party and the Republic's two Communist organizations: the Dominican Communist party and the Popular Socialist party.

Although industrial and labor groups are beginning to gain power in the Republic, the military is by far the most powerful sector of society. The armed forces include an army of 14,000, an air force of 6,000, and a navy of 4,500. Military influence on matters of state has increased rather than decreased since Trujillo's death.

The only other important political power in the Republic is the Roman Catholic church, which extends its influence over the people through its involvement in social programs such as health care, housing, and labor relations.

Economy, Transportation, Communication

The Dominican economy has always relied heavily on agriculture. Today, half of the work force is involved in farming. Forty percent of Dominicans are farmers, while another 10 percent make their living in farm-related industry. Recently, however, the Republic has also begun mining its mineral reserves, tapping some of its natural resources, developing light industry, and building resorts to attract tourists.

Few Dominican farmers actually own land. Most of them are tenant farmers or sharecroppers. More than half the farms in the Republic are owned by the government. Many others are owned by wealthy Dominicans or by American corporations. The government has attempted to increase land ownership by Dominican farmers, but little progress has been made. Those who are lucky enough to own land usually have less than five acres and can grow only enough to feed their own families. As a result, many farm people have moved to the cities in search of work.

*Tobacco plantations produce
one of the major export crops*

The Republic's chief export is sugar cane. The country yields an average of 11 million metric tons of sugar each year. The sugar industry employs 85,000 Dominicans and produces almost half of the Republic's export earnings. But it does not pay well: a man must harvest three tons of cane a day to earn the equivalent of only about four United States dollars. Low wages have caused many Dominicans to stay away from the sugar industry. Labor must be imported from neighboring Haiti, where unemployment is very high. The Haitian sugar cutters are housed in government-owned shacks, called *bateys*, surrounding the sugar fields.

Other significant export crops include coffee, cocoa beans, and tobacco. Crops for domestic consumption include rice, beans, cassava (a grain that is the source of tapioca), and plantains (tropical fruits that resemble bananas). The diet of most Dominicans relies heavily on these few locally grown crops and is poor in meat. The country has only about 2.2 million beef cattle and fewer than 250,000 dairy cows, providing the average Dominican with about 5 ounces (145 grams) of meat per week and .33 pint (.15 liter) of milk per day. Pig farming was developed in the late 1970s in order to combat the country's meat deficiency, but an epidemic of swine fever wiped out the pig population and ended Dominican pork production.

Natural Resources

The Dominican Republic contains a surprising number of natural resources. Surveys have shown modest reserves of bauxite, nickel, silver, and gold. Because the nation's economy has been largely agricultural, many of these resources have yet to be mined. Recently, however, United States companies have moved into the country to conduct mining operations. Now, mining accounts for nearly 4 percent of the Republic's export income.

Bauxite, used in making aluminum, is mined at Cabo Rojo near the Haitian border. The bauxite reserves are controlled by the Aluminum Corporation of America (ALCOA), which has been mining them since the late 1950s. Because of an overabundance of aluminum, however, bauxite production has been drastically cut, and many workers have lost their jobs. Several mines have lain dormant since the late 1970s. Despite this slowdown, scientists estimate that only a 30-year supply of bauxite remains.

Nickel is more abundant. Used to make stainless steel, it is extracted from huge, open-pit mines in the center of the Republic. At present, nickel mining provides jobs for more than 2,000 Dominicans, who earn the equivalent of more than three United States dollars per hour. The Canadian-owned Falconbridge Nickel Corporation controls Dominican nickel reserves.

On the outskirts of Cotui, the government-owned Rosario Dominica Company produces "gold bricks"—metal blocks that are actually 25 percent gold and 75 percent silver—at the rate of 1,000 ounces per day. Rosario Dominica currently produces about $47 million (U.S.) worth of gold bricks each year and employs 730 Dominicans. When the company began operations, American interests owned 80 percent of its assets and the Republic only 20 percent. Because the project has been successful, the government recently decided to buy out another 26 percent.

A Dominican laborer straddles a palm tree to harvest coconuts

Geological studies performed in the early 1980s indicate that the Dominican Republic may have vast oil reserves. An oil field has been discovered outside Barahona in the southwest, and the government now plans to drill more. Estimates claim that the Barahona field alone may meet half the country's petroleum needs.

Another notable resource, natural gems provide the basis for jewelry making, one of the Republic's cottage industries. Amber, a clear, rock-like substance that is capable of burning, is mined in the mountains by Dominican men and boys, who chip out the substance with chisels, hammers, and picks. Until the beginning of the 19th century, no one knew that amber was not a stone. Actually, amber is a fossil resin (sap from plants or trees) formed millions of

57

Jewelry made from polished amber is a popular tourist souvenir

years ago. It ranges in color from bright yellow to black, but is most often gold-colored. Many pieces have natural objects such as spiders or flies trapped inside them. Although amber can be used as fuel, it is most often polished to a high gloss and set in gold or silver jewelry. Amber jewelry is one of the country's most popular tourist souvenirs.

The Republic is also famous for handcrafted jewelry made from native *larimar*, a light blue stone also known as Dominican Turquoise and found only in the Dominican Republic. Dominicans like to mount larimar stones with wild boar's teeth.

One of the Republic's untapped resources is its forests. The wide variety of trees found there could provide the country with a lively and profitable export trade. Unfortunately, much of the forestland lies miles from the nearest paved roads, so logging is difficult. And the abundant reserves have dwindled rapidly within the past several decades. Squatters (people who illegally settle on land they do not own) and small farmers have recklessly chopped down entire forests. In the 1960s, the government outlawed such careless logging and instituted reforestation programs. Unfortunately, many formerly wooded tracts are still barren.

At one time, much of the country's mahogany was used to build Spanish ships. But, as wooden ships became outdated, mahogany logging was drastically reduced. Today, mahogany is no longer an important source of income for the Republic. It has been named the national tree, however, in honor of its former importance.

Still another natural resource is fish. Offshore waters are rich in mullet, mackerel, red snapper, shrimp and kingfish. But fishing makes only a small contribution to the nation's economy. Most of the 12,000 tons of fish caught each year are eaten locally and not exported.

Miles of beaches have helped Dominicans build a brisk tourist trade

Industry

Industry contributes only 15 percent of Dominican revenue. Two-thirds of all manufacturing is related to the food industry, and other light industry is beginning to develop. The Republic now produces enough clothing, cement, and cardboard to meet its needs. More than half the chemical fertilizers used on Dominican farms are also manufactured in the country.

Still, the Republic must import most of its consumer goods. Cars, chemicals, appliances, and even food products come from the United States. And, although Dominican oil production is increasing, nearly one-quarter of the country's total import bill is paid to Mexico and Venezuela for petroleum.

Tourism

Although it has a tropical climate and miles of beaches, the Dominican Republic was neglected by tourists until recently. While Trujillo ruled, foreigners were decidedly unwelcome. In the decades since his assassination, however, the Republic's leaders have made an effort to attract American and European travelers to their country. With the help of United States firms, the Dominicans have built a tourist trade that contributes more than one-third of the nation's revenue.

The Republic's southern coast has undergone a transformation in the last several years. Puerto Plata and Sousa, two coastal towns, have recently been renovated to attract visitors. The sleepy coastal village of La Romana has been turned into a major vacation resort. The Hotel Romana, perched on 270 acres of beachfront overlooking the Caribbean, is a favorite of American tourists. Originally a small guest house, the hotel was converted into a resort complex by American architect William Cox. Another of La Romana's resorts, the Casa de Campo, is located on a golf course.

Santo Domingo is also attracting tourists. Hotels such as El Embajador, Cervantes, and the Hotel Santo Domingo have recently been built to accommodate visitors to the Western Hemisphere's oldest city. Dominican leaders have capitalized on the city's history and ideal location—overlooking the Caribbean Sea—to create a brisk tourist trade.

Currency

As late as the 1940s, the Dominican Republic had no currency of its own. Because of the nation's close economic ties to the United States, American money was used throughout the country. In 1947, however, the Republic adopted the peso as its unit of currency. Until 1983, one peso was worth one U.S. dollar; since then, its worth has dropped to only 40 U.S. cents.

Tourists can visit this restored citadel

A row of cannons protected this 16th-century fort from pirate raids

Transportation

The Dominican Republic has about 7,500 miles (12,000 kilometers) of roads, many of them unpaved. Some rural roads are very treacherous—travelers must be prepared for potholes and places where the roads have been washed out by heavy rain.

In the cities, however, modern roadways have been built. A major highway connects Santo Domingo to the nation's second largest city, Santiago. Taxis and buses are common sights on the city streets. But only the wealthiest Dominicans own automobiles. Most of the cars on the highways have been rented by tourists.

The Dominican Republic also has a railway system. Railroads are used primarily for industrial purposes, carrying loads of sugar from inland cane fields to the refineries and ports on the coast.

Of the many seaports, the most important are Santo Domingo, on the Caribbean coast, and Puerto Plata, serving Santiago and the Cibao Valley on the Atlantic coast. Outside Santo Domingo, an international airport offers direct flights to the United States, Venezuela, Colombia, and various Caribbean islands. A second international airport was recently built on the outskirts of Puerto Plata.

Communications

The Dominican Republic has always had a lively communications system. In the late 1800s, scores of newspapers and magazines were published in Santo Domingo and Santiago. The Santiago daily *El Dia* (The Day) was first published in 1891. *Listin Diario* (Listin Diary), an early Santo Domingo paper, had a circulation of more than 1,000 in 1893. There were also many tabloids with sensational names such as *Cojanlo* (Grab It) and *La Bomba* (The Bomb). In the late 19th century, Dominicans kept abreast of local gossip by reading these scandal sheets. Today, the Republic has ten daily newspapers. It also has 105 radio stations and 4 television stations.

The first telephone conversation in the Dominican Republic took place in Santo Domingo in 1886. Within two years, a telephone network began to develop throughout the country. Today, telephone service links all major points.

Oddly, the telegraph did not come to the Republic until after the telephone. Legal and economic problems prevented full telegraph installation until the mid-1890s, but today telegraph systems exist throughout the country.

Santo Domingo and Other Cities

Santo Domingo, the capital of the Dominican Republic, is located in the south-central region of the country, on the Caribbean coast. It is the economic, cultural, and political hub of the nation. Its busy harbor receives most of the Republic's imports and ships most of its sugar and other exports. The more than 976,000 people (about 16 percent of the country's population) who live there make Santo Domingo more populous than Washington, D.C.

Santo Domingo is the oldest city in the Western Hemisphere, and many of its buildings are examples of Spanish Renaissance architecture. During the past four centuries, many of these old structures have fallen into disrepair. The government has restored much of Santo Domingo, however, and the ancient Colonial Zone, site of Bartolome Columbus's original settlement, has been totally renovated.

The Colonial Zone is still enclosed by the remains of its 15th-century stone wall. The narrow streets, old forts, and brightly colored buildings of old Santo Domingo have been restored so authentically that visitors almost expect to run into Diego de Valasque, Ponce de Leon, Hernan Cortes, and the other Spanish explorers who visited the city centuries ago.

This old fort is typical of Santo Domingo's Colonial Zone

Old and modern Santo Domingo meet at the Parque Independencia (Independence Park), a large square where the three fathers of the country are buried. These men—Duarte, Sanchez and Mella—led the Republic's fight for freedom from Haiti in 1884. A shrine called the Altar de la Patria marks their graves. The Parque Independencia is a popular meeting place on weekend afternoons. Old men sit in the hot sun playing dominoes, and young couples watch the steady stream of passersby.

At the entrance to the square is El Conde Gate, named for Count (El Conde) de Pensalva, a Dominican governor who resisted British forces in the 19th century. The gate was also the site of the March for Independence that ended Haitian domination of the Republic in 1844.

Colonial architecture gives Santo Domingo old-world charm

Along nearby El Conde Street is Columbus Square, built to honor the man who discovered the island. It contains a large statue of Christopher Columbus, sculpted in 1897 by French artist Gilbert. The square is a popular meeting place for Dominicans and a well-known tourist attraction.

Columbus Square is the site of the Cathedral of Santa Maria la Menor, the oldest cathedral in the New World. Built in 1514, the gold-and-coral limestone structure is an exquisite example of Spanish Renaissance architecture. In the 450-year-old sanctuary, 4 columns resembling palm trees support a marble sarcophagus (stone coffin) that is said to contain the bones of Christopher Columbus himself.

Dominican silver covers the altar of Cathedral de Santa Maria la Menor, and the cathedral contains many priceless works of art by great Renaissance masters. The most notable are a painting of the Madonna by the Spanish artist Bartolome Esteban Murillo, silver bells created by the famous Italian metalsmith and sculptor Benvenuto Cellini, and an emerald-studded crown that was once worn by Spain's Queen Isabella. In 1979, Pope John Paul II made a special visit to the cathedral to see its ornate altars and shrines.

The most outstanding structure in the old city is the Alcazar, a splendid, early-16th-century palace overlooking the winding Ozoma River. Built for Diego Columbus, Christopher's son, the Alcazar is made of Dominican coral limestone. For 60 years after its construction, the palace was the center of the Spanish court, which entertained many explorers, noblemen, and wealthy Europeans. When the Spanish colony fell on hard times in the early 17th century, the Alcazar was abandoned. By the 19th century, it was in ruins. During the Trujillo years, however, the Alcazar was restored to its original splendor. Today, visitors can admire the palace's beautiful architecture and its 24 rooms decorated with priceless paintings, tapestries, and antiques.

The capital city also has the oldest stone house in the Western Hemisphere, the Casa del Cordon, or House of the Cord. Located in the shadow of the Alcazar, it was named for the cord belts worn by the Franciscans, Roman Catholic monks who built the Casa in the 16th century.

Casa del Cordon played an important role in Dominican history. In an official capacity, it housed the first Superior Court of

Built for Diego Columbus, the Alcazar is made of Dominican limestone

Justice in the entire West Indies. In 1586, the Casa was the site of a less official but equally historic event. When Sir Francis Drake overran the island in that year, he ordered the wealthy women of Santo Domingo to bring their jewelry to Casa del Cordon, where he stored his booty until he left the island. A Dominican bank, the Banco Popular Dominicano, recently paid to have Casa del Cordon renovated.

Modern Santo Domingo

In startling contrast to the Colonial Zone is nearby modern Santo Domingo. The new sections of the city—known for palm-shaded boulevards and many restaurants, hotels, and nightclubs—were built by President Trujillo after the 1930 hurricane leveled the capital.

In the new downtown area, Dominicans can now visit President Trujillo's former national palace. Built in 1939, this three-story, domed structure has been the seat of government since 1947. Concerts are sometimes held in its landscaped gardens. Because the first floor still contains government offices, visitors are only allowed on the upper two floors, where many remnants of the Trujillo era—including the former dictator's immense, velvet-upholstered chair—are displayed. On the third floor of the palace is the Hall of Caryatides—a large room supported by 44 Greek-style columns—and the presidential suite, which once housed foreign dignitaries. Visitors are especially impressed by the amount of marble used in the palace.

Another important attraction in the modern capital is the Plaza

Dominicans can now visit Trujillo's former national palace

de la Cultura. Located on the former site of Trujillo's private mansion, the Plaza contains the National Library, the National Theater, and the Gallery of Modern Art. The National Theater sponsors folk dancing, opera, art exhibits, music concerts, and classical ballet performances. The Gallery of Modern Art contains an impressive collection of national and international paintings. A short walk away is the Paseo de los Indios, a 5-mile-long (8-kilometer) park containing fountains and an artificial lake.

The Dominican government wants to make Santo Domingo a major Caribbean resort. The city now has several luxury hotels, and tourists find that prices in the Dominican Republic are lower than those in many other Caribbean vacation spots. Government incentives have also encouraged the opening of many exceptional restaurants. Local specialties include *sancocho*, a thick stew made with meats, vegetables, and herbs, and *chicharrones de pollo*, a dish of chicken and green bananas deep-fried and flavored with pungent spices.

69

*Built in the colonial style, this
modern resort draws tourists*

Progress and Problems

The government has succeeded in modernizing the capital and
making it comfortable for tourists. Unfortunately, Santo Domingo is
not as comfortable for its native population. In the past 20 years,
rapid population growth has created many problems for the city.

Trujillo's government made it unlawful for people to move
from one part of the country to another. People from the Dominican interior were not allowed to move to the cities, and city-
dwellers were forbidden to take up residence in the country. After
Trujillo's death in 1961, however, Santo Domingo was flooded
with farmers who could no longer find land in the rural areas and
wanted to start new lives in the capital. The city's population dou-
bled in seven years. Unfortunately, most of these farm people could
not find good jobs. Many peasants who had come to seek their
fortunes were forced to live in slums so dangerous that even the
police were afraid to venture into them.

The rapid growth of Santo Domingo put a tremendous strain
on the city's water system. Much of the water became undrinkable

because of poor sewage treatment, and shortages were common. By the 1980s, the sewage problem had become so serious that untreated waste was being funneled directly into the Caribbean. The government, plagued by inadequate funding, is still struggling with the city's water problems.

Santiago

Santo Domingo's only metropolitan rival is Santiago, a city of 200,000 located in the north-central Republic in the middle of the fertile Cibao Valley. Santiago (also known as Santiago de los Caballeros) has built an economy around farming and farm-related industry.

The city's chief industry is cigar manufacturing, using tobacco grown on nearby plantations. Another important industry is rum manufacturing. Because Santiago's economy depends heavily on the export of rum and cigars, many Dominicans refer to it as a "sin economy."

The interior courtyard of a Dominican monastery

Puerto Plata and Other Towns

Another important Dominican town is Puerto Plata. Although not a major city, it is gaining fame as a tourist resort. Since the mid-1970s, the government has built a seaside parkway, a resort colony, and housing developments in Puerto Plata. These modern features blend with colonial architecture to make the city one of the prettiest in the Republic. Streets in the Old Town are lined with Victorian-style houses decorated with ornate, wrought-iron railings. This old-world charm, together with modern conveniences, make Puerto Plata appealing to tourists.

Located on a beautiful, U-shaped bay 17 miles (27 kilometers) west of Puerto Plata is Sousa. During the 1930s and 1940s, Sousa became a haven for Jews fleeing Nazi Germany. Most of the Republic's Jews live there today. The tiny port city is now being developed as a vacation resort.

A number of other coastal towns have also been developed as resorts. Once-sleepy fishing villages such as La Romana and Las Calderas are now crowded with hotels and vacationers. Small towns are likely to keep growing as the government continues to encourage tourism and economic development.

Cultural Life

Spanish, African, and West Indian customs and beliefs combine to create a uniquely Dominican culture. Each of these ethnic influences can be seen in Dominican music, dance, literature, and art.

Dominicans love music. The rhythms and melodies of Dominican folk music reflect both African and Spanish influences. Folk songs, called *decimas*, are little poems—usually about love—set to the music of guitars and native percussion instruments called *maracas, palitos* and the *guira*. A music society in Santo Domingo is dedicated to collecting and studying these folk songs.

Classical music is also known and loved in the Republic. The National School of Fine Arts trains young Dominicans in classical performance and orchestration. The most talented musicians aspire to perform with the National Symphony Orchestra.

Dance is a Dominican passion. The *merengue*, a ballroom dance characterized by a stiff-legged, limping step, is considered the national dance. The merengue is danced to songs with lyrics about love, the beauty of the countryside, or politics. Many other popular dances exhibit a strong Spanish influence. The *yuca*, the *sarambo*, the *guarapo*, the *zapateo*, and the *fandango* have been danced by Dominicans since the 19th century.

Many Dominican folk dances exhibit a strong Spanish influence

Over the years the Dominican Republic has produced many notable writers. Among the best-known are members of the Henriquez-Ureña family. Salomé Ureña de Henríquez (1850-1897) was a respected poet who in 1881 established the Instituto de Señoritas (the Women's Institute), the Republic's first center of higher learning for women. Her two sons were brilliant writers as well.

Pedro Henríquez-Ureña (1884-1946) was a critic, teacher, and philologist (one who studies languages and their history) noted for his association with Mexican writer and philosopher José Vasconcelos. In the 1920s, the two worked on improving education in Mexico. Later, Pedro became the director of the Institute of Philology in Buenos Aires, Argentina. During the 1940s, he gave a series of lectures at Harvard University in Cambridge, Massachusetts. These lectures were later published as *Literary Currents in Hispanic America*. He also wrote a famous history book on Spanish-American culture. One of the Republic's four universities is named after him.

Pedro's brother, Max Henríquez-Ureña (1883-1968), was a literary critic and a cultural historian. His books include a history of modern Spanish-American literary trends and a survey of Dominican literature. Max taught at major universities throughout Latin America and the United States.

Other important Dominican writers include Gaston Fernando Delingue (1861-1913), often called the Dominican national poet; Fabio Fiallo (1886-1942), the author of many beautiful love poems; Manuel de Jesús Galván (1834-1910), the author of *Enriquillo*, a novel based on an Indian revolution against the Spanish settlers; and Manuel del Cabral, whose works reflect a strong black influence. Modern writers include former President Juan Bosch, an essayist, novelist and short-story writer, and E. Rodriguez Deomorozi, a noted historian.

Although fine arts are taught at the National School of Fine Arts in Santo Domingo, the country is most noted for its folk art. Striking wood carvings made of mahogany are a uniquely Dominican art form. These handcrafted treasures are sold at markets around the capital city.

Santo Domingo's Cultural Plaza shows that the fine arts are important to the Republic. In addition to a museum of Dominican history, the Plaza contains a Gallery of Modern Art, a National Library and a National Theater. Plans are underway to create additional cultural centers.

75

Education

The Education Act of 1951 made education compulsory for all Dominican children between the ages of 7 and 14, but schooling has been hindered by a shortage of qualified teachers, poor facilities, and an overwhelmingly large school-age population. For thousands of children who have to work to support their families, schooling ends after four or five years. More than half of the population cannot read or write.

The government is trying to eliminate illiteracy and promote education. During the 1970s, President Joaquín Balaguer spent millions of dollars to improve schools and teachers. Unfortunately, Balaguer's millions were not enough. A typical rural school has nearly 300 students and only 3 teachers. Although each teacher is responsible for about 100 students, average salaries equal only about $90 (U.S.) a month.

Although the government has established a public school system, private or religious schools have always been necessary for gifted students. Students who continue their education after the sixth grade must travel to a school in one of the large cities. Unfortunately, private schools are expensive, and only the children of the wealthy can afford to advance to the higher grades.

Students stand at attention in front of this military academy

There are four colleges in the Dominican Republic. The National University in Santo Domingo is not only the oldest college in the Republic, it is also the oldest in the New World. Established in 1538, it is noted for its school of medicine. Pedro Henríquez-Ureña University, a public institution named for the famous Dominican author, has a school for tropical agriculture. The Instituto Superior de Agricultura in Santiago is the nation's top agricultural school, and the Universidad Catolica Madre y Maestra, a Catholic university, was the first college in the Republic to grant engineering degrees.

Illiteracy is tied to the nation's economic woes. Before education can improve, the standard of living must rise. Despite the Dominican Republic's problems, however, its literacy rate is higher than it has ever been, and the government is doing all it can to provide education for its people.

Baseball great Juan Samuel of the Philadelphia Phillies got his start in the port city of San Pedro de Macoris

Recreation

Life in the Dominican Republic is vigorous and pulsating, both by day and at night. Swimmers and sun worshippers enjoy the country's Caribbean beaches. Sportsmen participate in such activities as snorkeling, golfing, and deep-sea fishing. Spectators attend baseball, horse racing, and cockfighting events. Tourists and Dominicans alike shop at the many outdoor markets and take part in the nightlife of the cities.

Like many of its Caribbean neighbors, the Republic is known for its magnificent beaches. But they are not as easy to get to as on some islands. Residents of the capital travel for 45 minutes to Boca Chica beach. Other beautiful beaches are even harder to reach: Puerto Plata is a difficult, three-hour drive from Santo Domingo, and La Romana on the southern coast is a two-hour trip. Community swimming pools have been built in Santo Domingo for those who cannot reach the beaches.

The Dominican Republic is also well-known for its virgin coral reefs, perfect for scuba divers and snorkelers. Divers can explore ancient shipwrecks, underwater gardens, and an endless array of aquatic life among the reefs, where the colorful coral gives the water a purple hue.

79

Dedicated golfers can choose among many golf courses. Playa Dorado, a lavish course outside Puerto Plata, was planned by famous golf course designer Robert Trent Jones. The Santo Domingo Country Club is for members only, but guests of the city's big hotels are occasionally granted playing privileges.

Serious fishermen may rent boats and try their hands at deep sea fishing. Prize-winning sailfish, dolphin, marlin, tuna, barracuda, and red snapper are regularly caught in the green and purple waters near the capital. Boats can be rented complete with crew, gear, bait, and refreshments.

By far the most popular recreation—for sportsman and spectator alike—is baseball. The country has produced an unusually large number of excellent ball players, many of whom have played in the major leagues. In fact, one Dominican town, San Pedro de Macoris, has the distinction of producing more professional baseball players than any other town in the world. Each year, major league baseball scouts from the United States descend on this port city 40 miles (64 kilometers) from Santo Domingo to recruit local players. Such baseball greats as Juan Samuel of the Philadelphia Phillies and Joaquín Andujar of the Oakland A's got their starts in San Pedro de Macoris.

Thousands of Dominican baseball fans attend important games, usually held at one of the large stadiums in Santo Domingo. Whereas the major league baseball season begins in April and lasts through October, the Dominican playing season is from October to February. This gives big-league scouts plenty of time to check out the talent in San Pedro de Macoris before the major league season begins.

Dominican baseball fans attend games at the Santo Domingo stadium

Another popular spectator sport is horse racing. Perla Antillana, Santo Domingo's race track, schedules races four days per week. Many Dominicans enjoy spending an entire day at the race track, eating lunch at the track restaurant and watching the horses run. Perla Antillana is also quite popular with tourists.

People unfamiliar with Latin American tradition may be surprised to learn of the popularity of cockfighting—a sport in which spectators bet on the outcome of a pecking match between two roosters. Although cockfighting is illegal in the United States and many other countries, it is a favorite diversion in many Latin American lands. Cockfights are held at the new Santo Domingo Cockfighting Coliseum. This modern complex has comfortable seats, air conditioning, and closed-circuit television.

81

Spanish style dominates this 16th-century desk

For those who are not sports-minded, the Dominican Republic offers plenty of opportunities for shopping, with bargains available all over the country. Prices can be especially low for shoppers who follow the Dominican custom of dickering with the merchants.

These merchants expect no one to pay the assigned price for an item. Instead, the customer must be prepared to negotiate a lower price for the merchandise he wants.

Any dedicated Dominican shopper is well-acquainted with the Mercado Modelo on Avenida Mella in Santo Domingo. Stalls at the Modelo overflow with fascinating crafts: tortoiseshell combs and trinkets, sandals, handwoven baskets, straw hats, and clay fish pots. The market is also abundantly stocked with fruits, vegetables, and spices. Because the Modelo is a major shopping center for Santo Domingo's residents, it is always crowded. Many tourists become lost among the winding stalls.

One special craft found at the marketplace is the handmade rocking chair. Ever since the Dominican government presented one as a gift to United States President John F. Kennedy, these wooden rockers have been extremely popular throughout the Republic. They are sold unassembled and must be put together by the customer.

Other bargains include ceramic pots, macramé (a coarse lace made by knotting cord or rope), hand-knit clothing, and of course, Dominican rum and cigars. Foreign shoppers must remember that market stalls are closed between 12:30 P.M. and 2 P.M., when shopkeepers take a *siesta*, or afternoon rest. The siesta is a custom in most Latin American (and many European) countries. Those who enjoy nightlife are not disappointed in the Dominican Republic. From old-fashioned nightclubs to discos to gambling casinos, the Republic has some of the most exciting after-dark activities in the Caribbean.

Santo Domingo is especially dynamic at night. One of the most unusual evening attractions in the Republic is the Meson de la Cueva, in the heart of the capital. Built 50 feet (15 meters) underground in a natural cave, the Meson is reached by descending a huge, freestanding iron staircase. Patrons sit at tables underneath huge stalactites (calcium deposits shaped like icicles) that hang from the roof of the cave.

Food at the Meson is recognized as the best in Santo Domingo. Guests dine on traditional Dominican fare such as *gazpacho* (a cold soup made of cucumbers, tomatoes, onions, and garlic). Fresh seafood from the local waters is always available. A favorite is fresh sea bass in red sauce. Other dishes include *tournedos*, small slices of beef served with a variety of sauces, and *coq au vin*, chicken stewed with red wine, diced pork, onions, and mushrooms. The club also offers live dance music and floor shows featuring traditional Dominican merengue dancing. After midnight, the Meson's waiters put on a show. Whereas many people go to the Meson de la Cueva for dinner, some go for the entertainment alone.

Another leading nightclub in the city is the Village Pub, located in the Colonial Zone. Known as one of the liveliest places in Santo Domingo, the Pub is a sprawling tropical garden with soaring trees and an immense screen that shows music videos. Near the entrance is an elegant parlor decorated with busts and old musical instruments.

Old-fashioned piano bars in many of the city's big hotels attract large crowds. Las Palmas, an exclusive club in the Hotel Santo Domingo, was decorated by world-famous fashion designer Oscar de la Renta, a native of the Dominican Republic. The bar overlooks the blue Caribbean Sea and adjoins a large outdoor terrace. Talented pianists perform jazz music for guests of Las Palmas.

Gambling is legal in the Republic, and Santo Domingo is noted for several major gambling casinos. The largest, El Embajador Casino, is a favorite of many Dominican high rollers. Open from 3 P.M. until 4 A.M., El Embajador offers blackjack, craps, and roulette. Gamblers wanting a break from the whirl of the roulette wheels can spend a moment at the adjoining bar.

Although many of the Dominican Republic's recreational, shopping, and nightlife activities appeal to tourists, they are enjoyed by Dominicans as well. Modern Dominicans need not restrict themselves to the home and workplace.

The Republic's many old buildings reveal its colonial past

The Dominican Republic Today

From its beginning nearly 500 years ago, the Dominican Republic has faced obstacles. Its people have struggled to establish democracy after centuries of foreign rule and decades of dictatorship. Class distinctions, racial discrimination, and poverty have made life

difficult for most people. Like many of its island neighbors in the Caribbean region, the Dominican Republic suffers serious economic and social problems.

Less than 25 years ago, most Dominicans lived in the country and worked on small family farms. Today, increasing numbers are moving to the big cities, particularly to Santo Domingo. Since the mid-1960s, the capital's population has grown from about 300,000 to almost 1,000,000. The city was unequipped for such a rapid influx of people. Much of the housing is substandard, water quality is poor, and rural peasants who came in search of work have found that job opportunities are scarce.

The Ozama River and the Caribbean Sea as seen from Homage Tower

87

Homage Tower, where Hispaniola's first governor imprisoned Christopher Columbus

Nevertheless, the Dominicans are struggling to better their country and their lives. Conditions have improved. Most important, the people finally have a voice in their government. The beautiful island that Columbus first sighted five centuries ago is beginning to fulfill its promise. The long traditions and deep faith of the Dominicans keep them fighting for freedom, equality and prosperity.

Index